COSPLAY ACADEMY

A guide for new cosplayers and veteran cosplayers alike

By

Harloe I. Hunter

Dedications

I dedicate this to My Mom and Dad for supporting me and my decision on being a cosplayer. I would also like to dedicate this to my cousin Mia, if it wasn't for you I would have never discovered the joys of cosplaying. I also want to dedicate this to all of Anime Ramen Pro's subscribers on YouTube and watchers on deviantArt.

Also thanks to all of my watchers on my MitsukiUzumaki21 deviantArt page, and all of my friends at Manatee School for the Arts. I love you all. I also want to dedicate this to Master William Kenneth Ellis. Though you may not be here physically, you are still here in my heart.

Acknowledgements

I want to give a giant bucket full of pocky and tons of other yummy Japanese candy to these amazing people who helped making Cosplay Academy a reality. Mia and Justin Reyes, my parents John and January Hunter, all of my friends from M.S.A and all the friends I've made at the conventions I've been to. I want to thank Peter Morlon for all his support in getting my book published. I want to thank Justin Rifner, for a wonderful job at editing my book, and supporting me and for just dealing with me no matter what.

. I also want to thank every cosplayer that reads this book. If you all weren't out there, then I could have never been inspired to write this book or even cosplay. I love you all so much, thanks for believing.

Cosplay Academy

Contents

- ♥ Loli-History

- ♥ Visual Kei and Loli-Fashion

Introductions

Hello, cosplayers. Welcome to Cosplay Academy, my name is Harloe also know as Neofang, founder of AnimeRamenProductions from youtube.com and I will be your guide through the wonderful, wacky world of cosplaying. I have heard this phrase from time to time from all those "anti-cosplayers" "You cosplay? That's so childish." Yeah....No, we cosplayers are not childish, well except for the running around cons and having fun part.

Along with these little comments from all these anti-cosplayers, are comments from parents of the younger cosplayers like, "Oh, cosplaying is just a phase; you'll grow out of it." Or "Cosplay is against our religion." Um, sure being a cosplayer maybe is a phase for most teens, but for the some of us it's not just a phase and it is in no way shape or form wrong in any religion. Cosplay is a way of life, and is also a way to express yourself. It's how most of us get out of the house, and meet new people and make friends who we cherish for the rest of our lives.

Now, I understand that most of us cosplayers just want to teach these anti-cosplayers that just because we love to dress up in weird costumes it doesn't make us queers or weirdoes. Well just as much as I would love to drag them to a con and show them that there is nothing wrong with cosplaying, I don't think you should doing that. Think about it, we are already labeled as "Childish" so no dragging your friends that don't have a fondnesss for cosplaying to a con okay? Good.

The reason for Cosplay Academy, is that most of our cosplayers are what I call "Closet Cosplayers" they just need a little boost to explore the world of Cosplay. You're all probably wondering "what in the world is a Closet Cosplayer?"

Well a Closet Cosplayer is what I call someone that isn't quite comfortable with being around others in costumes, can't ever leave their homes because they aren't able to drive, they aren't old enough to go to cons or parents won't let them go because they think it's a waste of time and money, it's against their religion, or they don't have any friends nearby that cosplay.

This is also a big deal in the anime community, and it's not just affecting cosplayers, but it also affects others too. Because of bullies, most cosplayers are afraid to express themselves because they fear that people will make fun of them. I see many people getting bullied for many different reasons, including cosplay, but hey if people want to make fun of cosplay they should know that it teaches us many useful skills. Some of those skills come in handy like sewing, painting, and learning to give into imagination, so they can go shove it.

Anyway, that is my reason for writing Cosplay Academy, so let's get on with this introduction.

Okay I know what you're thinking now, "just who the hell is NeoFang anyway and why is she telling us this stuff?" Well I'm telling you this because, I think it would be a good way to explain what cosplay is and hopefully motivate more people to do it and tell them how. Okay enough of that, I guess I should tell you who I am.

For starters, my name is Harloe Hunter; I have been a cosplayer since elementary school, and the reason I started cosplaying was because of my cousins. They showed me all of these pictures of anime characters and made me watch anime shows and I instantly fell in love with the whole idea of being a cosplayer/anime fan. Ever since then I have been making all of my cosplays, I have only ever bought one cosplay, anf it was my Sebastian Michaelis cosplay from

Black Butler, because I couldn't find a tailcoat pattern.
Anyway getting off track, my first con was MetroCon
2008. My first cosplay for that con was Hinata Hyuuga
from Naruto. I have been going to cons for almost five
years now and I don't plan to stop yet.

Then two years later after I started middle school that's
when Anime Ramen Productions was born. Well it wasn't
called AnimeRamenPro just yet; we first started with the
name Dark Crystal Pro, and later changed it to Fun with
Cosplayers Pro. We still didn't like the name, so then I
came up with Anime Ramen Pro and we've stuck with it
ever since.

Anime Ramen Pro started with my cousins,
Akatsuki4evermore and my childhood friend
RosarioMoka22, best friend from middle school
Chiyomiyuki. As we grew, some of us left for certain

reasons which we'll leave out. Then we gained new members. If you watch us on YouTube then you know KyuubiKC, and another member CIEL. Our latest member is named Pteros (tehr-ohs). My Cosplaying name originally was FoolsHearts. I had that name for a year, but then later decided that I no longer liked the name so I changed it to MitsukiUzumaki21, hence the name from my deviantArt account. I stuck with that name for a year and half, and changed it to Black Fang. I did it because ,I've never cosplayed Mitsuki from Full Moon and Two; I don't really cosplay Naruto Uzumaki anymore. But then, since I am very picky about names, I later changed to NeoFang, which I've stuck with until this point.

Ok so now that introductions are over with, I'm gonna say what everyone reading this is thinking, "Gosh NeoFang, why did you decide to write this book anyway. What do you get out of this?" The reason I wrote this book was because I get asked a lot of questions about cosplaying from a lot of my friends, and first time cosplayers that I meet at cons. "What do you think would be a good first cosplay?" Or "where can I get a good quality wig?" "What type of fabric should I use or how much," etc…etc. I normally don't have a hard time answering everyone, so I thought that maybe putting all this information in a book would be a much better idea. So that way instead of sharing this with one person and then repeating myself over and over again, everyone can check the book and get the same information from it. "What do I get out of this?" Well it makes me feel accomplished that I'm able to share this information with all of you, and in doing so I'm finally letting out all this built up knowledge that I've wanted to spread for five years.

I guess I should mention what subjects we'll be going over in this book. There will be a wide variety of subjects mentioned in this book, but we'll mostly be going over…

- ♥ Cosplay History
- ♥ Types of Cosplayers
- ♥ Types of Lolitas
- ♥ What to Do and What Not to Do At Cons
- ♥ Tips for First time Con-goers
- ♥ Cosplay Construction
- ♥ Make up tips
- ♥ Wig Construction

Etc…

Now with all of that covered, let's enter the amazing and fantastic world of Cosplay. Now a word of warning, when reading this book each chapter will have sections and each section will have subsections. I'm not trying to confuse you; I just felt that things should be organized that way.

Chapter One

Hello and welcome to the first chapter, and the very

first step in our journey through cosplay. In this chapter I

will be going over the basics of cosplay history, like how

cosplay started, where it actually came from, how cosplay

is today, and its purpose. We will also be going over how to

deal with parents and friends that aren't supportive. This

topic is very important for cosplayers starting out. Also,

how to tell if you are a fan girl/boy. I know this topic seems

silly, but hey might as well make sure.

A brief History lesson on Cosplay

I've heard this so many times since I became I

cosplayer, "What is Cosplay?" That's a fine question

indeed. Literally speaking Cosplay or as the Japanese say

Kosupure (コスプレ), is a contraction of the words

"costume" and "play." People who take part in cosplay are

known as "cosplayers" or in Japan simply reyazu (レヤズ)
for "players."

So, "What is Cosplay exactly?" Well, cosplay is the act
of dressing up as your favorite character from animes,
videogames, mangas, movies, books, and even Visual-Kei
rock bands in Japan. Don't confuse cosplay for Halloween
costumes though, because they're <u>not</u> the same. Typically,
more time is spent on a cosplay costume because they are
normally made by the wearer. Also, in cosplay much more
attention is spent on detail.

Now you know what cosplay is, but in case you're not
sure how it got its name the term "cosplay" was coined by
Nov Takahashi in 1984, while attending a sci-fi convention
in Los Angeles. He was so impressed by the costume
masquerade that he wrote about it in Japanese sci-fi
magazines. Word spread quickly through Japan of this new

performance art. And the rest is history. Many people believe cosplay started in Japan, but that's not necessarily true. Forrest J. Ackerman inspired fan-costuming worldwide when he wore the first futuristic costume, made by Myrtle R. Douglas, to the 1st World Science Fiction Convention in 1939, in Caravan Hall, in New York.

Since then cosplay has spread to countries across the globe, like the Philippines, China, Italy, France, Mexico, Brazil, North America, Japan and the list continues. Despite the many impressive creations that come out of all these places, Japan is the largest exporter of quality cosplay. Why? Because, Japanese cosplay has taken cosplay to a new level.

They've managed to turn it into an art form, inspiring fellow cosplayers worldwide. (Not to mention making something as geeky as dressing up like cartoon characters look kind of cool.) It's no wonder most cosplayers, who have acquired celebrity status for their creations, hail from Japan.

Cosplay Today

Cosplayers today, Meet-up from time to time at places called Cons (or Anime Conventions). We meet up with other cosplayers outdoors throughout the weekend and pose for pictures and check out each other's awesome creations. During huge gatherings at cosplay cons they participate in masquerades, Question and Answer panels, skits, and contests.

Today the most popular fandoms at cons seem to be Naruto cosplays, Disney cosplays, Vocaloid cosplays, Blue Exorcist cosplays, DreamWorks cosplays, Avatar cosplays, Hetalia cosplays, Dr.Who cosplays, and Supernatural cosplays, BBC Sherlock Cosplays, and Homestuck cosplays. Films like Harry Potter and Lord of the Rings are a favorite among cosplayers and now of course The Dark Knight, who's Joker has become increasingly awesome to dress like.

Purpose

The cosplayer's purpose may generally be sorted into one of three categories. Most cosplayers draw characteristics from all three categories.

The first is to express adoration for a character, or in feeling similar to a character in personality, seeking to become that character. This type of cosplayer may be associated with being a Fan (person) and is often labeled as an Otaku.

Cosplayers are most likely to adopt the character's personality and are known to criticize other cosplayers for not

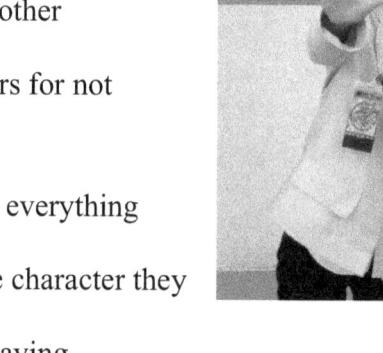

knowing everything about the character they are cosplaying.

The second are those people who enjoy the attention that cosplaying a certain character brings. Within the cultures of anime and manga specifically, as well as science fiction and fantasy, there is a certain level of fame that is attached to cosplayers. Such cosplayers are usually characterized by attention to detail in their cosplays and their choice of popular characters. They are also noted by

participation in cosplay competitions.

The third are

those who enjoy

the creative

process, and the

sense of personal

achievement

upon completion.

Such people are

more likely to

have a greater

budget dedicated to the project, more complicated and

better quality outfits with access to more materials.

They are also more likely to engage with professional photographers and cosplay photographers to take high quality images of a cosplayer in their cosplay posing as the character.

Well, that's the history of cosplay in a nutshell ^_^. Now that's over with let's move on shall we?

How could I tell if I'm a cosplayer/fan girl?

Now you're all probably wondering "how would I know if I'm a cosplayer or a Fan girl/Fan boy". Some people will tell you that you're just going with the latest trends. Well it should be a pretty simple answer, but it would still be too soon to tell. To discover if you might have an anime mindset, you have to look at the "symptoms." Why don't we check this list?

♥ A love for dressing up in elaborate costumes

♥ A knack for sewing

♥ Spend hours watching anime

♥ Reading manga instead of normal books

♥ Sometimes taking on the personality of a favorite

character

♥ Spend hours on youtube watching cosplay skits

♥ A love of being in front of a camera either for a

photo shoot or for a skit

- ♥ A love for video gaming for hours with friends
- ♥ Drawing styles having a hint trace of Manga style

I could go on and on with this list, but I won't. Now keep in mind that not every single cosplayer out there must like every single thing on this list. They could but that's up to them. So if you have a friend that has these traits, then introduce him/her to cosplay, if you haven't already. Now you probably notice that one of the traits is taking on the personality of a favorite character.

What that means is that you start acting like the character naturally. It happens to a lot of long time cosplayers, including me. I mean every new school year I have a new personality, but not everyone is like that. You don't have to have a character personality, though it's fun to have one ^_^.

That doesn't mean you have to style your hair the same or dye it the same color as the character, or dress the same way. Taking on the personality of a character comes naturally, when cosplayers fall in love with a character. If you do decide you want to take on a personality, be sure not to take it too far. You don't have to go all out, because then things will start to get awkward trust me.

Another thing you all probably noticed is that another trait on this list is your drawing style has a hint of manga art style. What I mean by that is that when you draw, your style becomes like a Japanese comic artist. Like for instance, the pictures in this book. All these picture were drawn by me and are all drawn manga style. Now you're all wondering "how could I develop a manga drawing style?" Well it's kind of simple, what I did was print a couple anime pictures and traced one and then take the others and try to draw it by looking at. But that's not the only way.

If you know someone that is a very good manga artist, you could ask them to teach you some tricks. I also did the same thing, I had my cousin show me some tricks, I have a lot of people tell me that I'm an amazing artist, but I am still learning.

Also another way to tell if you're an otaku is if you use some Japanese words in your sentences. Believe me I hear it all the time, like when you answer someone you hear the word "Hai" which means "yes" or "Nani" which means "what" or even "Sugoi" which means "great." Now you don't need to go and use Japanese in every day conversations. If you did no one who isn't an otaku or that isn't Japanese would be able to understand you. So be careful with how much Japanese you use in your conversations.

HELP!! I'm a Cosplayer, and My Friends think I'm a Freak

When you decide to be a cosplayer, you must understand that if you have friends that are not interested in the whole idea of watching anime for hours and going to cons with other cosplayers, they will think you're weird. Just because your friends think it's weird, doesn't mean you should stop cosplaying because of it. They will just have to get used to the idea of you being someone that likes to dress up with others from time to time at Anime Gatherings.

Even though you want to share your love of anime with every single one of your friends, you should keep in mind that some of your friends might not like hearing all that anime talk. I know, I know it's shocking that they don't want to hear you talk about the latest chapter of a manga series you started reading. Let's face it, not everyone is like you. If you really want to share this love of anime with your friends, well then be my guest; just remember to take it slow.

When I mean "take it slow" I mean show your friends one show or manga at a time, don't go crazy and give them a huge list of series to watch/read. You might just overload their brains, so I say again "take it slow" I'm sure they'll come around soon enough ^_^. I mean sometimes you will have a friend that thinks your hobby, which in this case is cosplaying, is interesting because we make all of our cosplays, or because we have the guts to go out in public and wear really exaggerated clothes.

One more thing you want to keep in mind, if you have a friend that just completely won't watch anime or doesn't want to cosplay, <u>don't push them to do it</u>!! Trust me, because the more you push them to cosplay or watch anime, the more you will push them away from the subject. Which would be bad and personally you don't want that. So please keep that bit of information in mind, besides making new friends at cons is much easier than trying to get your friend to watch Katekyou Hitman Reborn.

Any way the point is, if your friends still don't want to give anime a try don't force them because the last thing you want to do is start a fight about the issue possibly ending the friendship. So let's move on.

Real Otaku Friends

Okay so, I know that every one of you reading this has at least one or two friends that do share the same interest. Friends that are willing to go to a con with you. Friends that are willing to do random stuff with you. But most importantly, friends that are always there for you, no matter what horrible time you're going through. Trust, me as much as you want your friends that aren't anime lovers to come and join those of us on the otaku side, which only has a 50/50 chance of happening it'd be easier to find friends who are already there.

The friends that do share this love are friends you should never leave hanging. Believe me, it took me a long time for me to realize that they were my true friends. They helped my through bad times, horrible times, and of course the good times >w<. I had been going through a really bad time, and had been dealing with a lot of stress.

But they were there supporting me and trying to comfort me as best as they could. So basically, just remember who your true friends are, because they will be with you for the rest of your life. Especially if they're otakus. We've got to stick together in this messed up world right?

My parents don't understand my love for cosplay

Parents are probably the worst to deal with about hobbies that you are fascinated with. I hear that parents disapprove about almost every hobby that doesn't fit into the "when I was your age we did this and that and blah blah blah," But cosplay gets hit the hardest. I've seen this on all the blogs from newbie cosplayers about parents not understanding their love and obsession for cosplaying. Believe me my parents were the same way when I was starting out.

I mean yes parents think that dressing up in costumes when it's not Halloween and going to conventions with strange people is strange and sometimes concerning. But your parents love you and even though they might not show it, they respect your choice to cosplay. They just are concerned that you might get bullied by your peers. Now all you young cosplayers reading this should sit with your parents and make them read this.

Here are some frequently asked questions from parents about cosplay:

- ♥ Q: What is Cosplay?
- ♥ A: Cosplay is a hobby which anime fans dress up as their favorite or popular anime, manga, or videogame character.
- ♥ Q: Isn't cosplay….a bit strange
- ♥ A: Well to an Outsider yes, but a lot of people who don't know about cosplay instantly conjure up stereotyped images of large men dressed in Star Trek uniforms wandering around pretending to scan one-another. While I'm pretty sure those people do exist out there, they are far from representative of the majority of people who enjoy

cosplaying. But during my adventures of being a cosplayer I have managed to make tons of friends who don't think its strange.

♥ Q: Girls dressing up as boys is against god.

♥ A: Okay first of all, girls aren't the only ones that dress up as the opposite sex, even guys that like to cosplay will dress up as girls! It's all for fun, it's not like we dress as the opposite sex when we are not at cons. Well except for those who actually enjoy cross dressing they may like to do that. But just because some cosplayers like to dress up as a guy or girl doesn't mean we're turning gay or lesbian. So parents, relax your child is not turning gay/lesbian.

♥ Q: Should teenagers have a job….if they want to cosplay

♥ A: Having a job is really the best thing for us cosplayers, especially if you make your own cosplays and fabric plus patterns for your cosplay are kind of expensive. Also you also have convention ticket prices, hotels, and transportation to pay for as well, so having a job is in every cosplayers best interest.(Meaning don't always think that your parents are going to buy all your cosplay needs.)

And so…For all you parents reading this always remember cosplay will not make your child gay, lesbian, or bisexual. Cosplay is a way for teens to express themselves, make new friends, and who knows maybe even find the love of their lives. But Parents reading, you are not the only ones. Even my parents had a hard time accepting cosplay; I mean my dad thought anime was a cult. Which, anime is most definitely <u>not</u> a cult!! So parents, if you're keeping your anime loving child from doing something he/she loves, please reconsider ^_^.

Okay cosplayers now if your parents are still not having a change of heart on cosplay, then maybe try persuading them with how cosplay can teach useful skills to you.

1. If you want to show your parents that cosplay teaches useful skills, show them that it teaches cosplayers to sew and create props and do many other things as well. Like for example, cosplay can teach them how to act when you think about it. What some cosplayers do is create skits to do at a convention panel or as a video on youtube, and so they have to practice writing and acting. I know cosplay taught me how to open up and have fun with people and close friends, and because of that I managed to make some of the best friends a cosplayer could ask for.

2. Another way to show them that cosplay is a good thing is that it is a better way to spend time and money, better than drinking, doing drugs, and even spending money on useless things that you don't need. Now don't get me wrong about that last part, I know that I have done the same thing. What can I say, we're all human. But as you read this I bet right now at least ten teenagers are probably out wasting their money on a ton of drinks.

3. Another way is if your parents are super religious and think that if they're child cosplays that they will turn gay, lesbian, bisexual, etc. Then you should try to prove them wrong by showing them that it's completely not the case. Many people have met their soul mates at conventions. Whether they're gay or straight, but no one has ever turned gay cause of cosplaying. Yes people were inspired to come out to their families, but that's because they were always afraid to tell them not because of cosplay in general.

Internet

Ok this part is just as important, the internet is a huge web of drama and internet trolls. I have dealt with all sorts of drama. Many people including cosplayers post on Facebook, twitter or Tumblr about all sorts of problems that are going on in their personal life. Believe me I've had my fair share of posting drama. So please keep the drama posting to a written old school dairy, please because half the stuff being posted anywhere is just filling the internet to the brim.

To be quite honest everyone is just tired of seeing it. Plus parents aren't really happy with all the drama that is being posted on there, because it's all bullcrap, and it leads to nothing but hurt feelings and cyber bullying. So please stop with the unnecessary drama. It makes no one happy and it makes you look like a major jerk. So just save the

trouble and don't do it.

NeoFang's Summary

Ok, so basically this chapter in a nutshell was about how, when, and where cosplaying came from. We also discussed that even though you have friends that don't share the same interests, you can share the love and try to get them to spread the love too. Just take it easy ok ^_^. Plus, we talked about remembering who your true friends are. Another thing we discussed was that even though cosplay may be strange to parents of new and young cosplayers parents admit cosplaying is a much better thing to spend time and money on than drinking and doing drugs. Now with the summary out of the way let's get started on the next chapter.

Chapter Two

Now that we are going into chapter two, I should tell you that this chapter is about what kind of traits a cosplayer should have, knowing these are very important for cosplayers. Also we'll go over the ten commandments of an anime otaku, and cosplayers inspiration. A cosplayers inspiration is the key to being a good cosplayer.

Traits cosplayers should have

Cosplayers, sometimes you'll notice that some cosplayers you meet will somewhat seem the same to you in personality. The reason for that is because we all have similar traits. In this section we will go over some traits.

Manners

♥ No matter where you are, you should never forget your
manners. Say excuse me when passing through a
crowded place; never forget to say please and thank
you. These are called magic words for a reason. These
may seem stupid to some people but they really do
work wonders. If you show people respect, people will
respect you back. Just because you're at anime
convention having fun is not an excuse to behave badly.
There are other people around you, don't be selfish,
think of others too.

Patience

♥ To people asking why you are in costume, what cosplay
is and things like that. Patience will also come in handy
when you're combing out the tangles of a very long
wig, when hunting for things needed for a certain

costume or when waiting for your costume to be done. Remember, patience is a must.^-^

Resourcefulness

♥ Resourcefulness is a key term in cosplay, which means having the ability to act effectively or imaginatively, especially in difficult situations. In a tight pinch? One must think quickly and be able to use things around them to solve the problem. For example, you need to make a part of a cosplay, like let's say the skulls on Grell Sutcliff's glasses chain and you have no clay to make the skulls for it. You could use fabric felt if you have some lying around. Not all cosplayers have money, so one should be resourceful and use all the available resources to the fullest. Less money spent, the happier your pockets and wallets will be ^-^

Focus

♥ You need focus to help you finish your props and cosplay pieces on time. Having focus also helps one to be in character. Cosplay is 50% costume and 50% role playing. Focus, along with passion and dedication binds the two together to make a successful cosplay. ^_^

Dedication

♥ When you are dedicated to your hobby, you'll find time for it no matter how busy you are. You'll find money for your costumes when you thought you were broke. If you really want to cosplay, you'll find a way to make it work. ^_^

Passion

♥ Passion means having love and feeling strongly for cosplay. Loving cosplay itself and not the fame you think it brings. Passion is what drives people to work better and harder. When you love what you are doing, a lot of things are possible. Passion gives one an eye for detail because of course you want everything to be perfect or nearly perfect when you become that character.

Friendly

♥ Friends are always a good thing to have and you can never have enough of them. Smile and be friendly. Having a lot of friends can be tiring but in a nice way, because you get to hang out with people who have the same interest as you. Plus having friends always makes a bad situation seem a lot less bad. Another plus is that you can borrow stuff from them too! If you need help with your costumes or props, they can help you out ^-^.

Confidence

♥ If you're too shy to show the world your costume then cosplaying is probably not for you. It takes a certain amount of confidence to walk around wearing the not usually accepted look. Yes, people will stare, they will point and they will laugh too. If your self-confidence is kinda low then you're probably going to get really affected with all the bad stuff. Believe in yourself! Be brave, if you don't believe in yourself then other people won't believe in you.

Ok knowing these traits will be helpful in your journey as a cosplayer. But aside from all this, the most important thing about being a cosplayer is to be yourself; otherwise you won't enjoy yourself at cons and being around other cosplayers. The best part of all this is having a good time with everyone you meet.

THE TEN COMMANDMENTS OF AN ANIME OTAKU!

Ok, this was something I found on deviantArt that was very true about being an Otaku/Cosplayer, so I thought I'd share this with all of you. Just as the title states these are the Ten Commandments of an Anime Otaku.

1. YOU SHALL ALWAYS BE PROUD THAT YOU ARE AN OTAKU.

Always be proud that you are doing something that makes you who you are and not just another follower in this world of ours. Always be proud that you can express yourself and not give a care in the world.

2. YOU SHALL NEVER DO THINGS THAT WILL DESTROY THE NAMES OF ANIMES AND THE NAMES OF OTAKUS.

Being a cosplayer/otaku is always being respectful of fellow otakus. So basically this means don't trash the name of anime or otakus. We want to show that otakus are respectful types of people and not just a teenage phase.

3. YOU SHALL NEVER CONSIDER CARTOONS AS ANIME.

This basically says it all, cartoons are not anime. Yes they are animated series but not "anime."

4. YOU SHALL NEVER BETRAY ANIME.

Just don't stop liking anime, because if you betray anime your basically just saying that you were just following what everyone else was doing and that you are just a follower.

5. YOU SHALL KNOW MORE THAN TEN ANIME SERIES.

If you really call yourself an otaku you must at least know more than ten shows. I mean how else would you know and cosplay all these characters.

6. YOU SHALL WATCH ANIME AND READ MANGA AS MUCH AS YOU CAN.

Just watch and read anime. Enough said.

7. YOU SHALL ALWAYS KNOW EVERY SINGLE DETAIL OF YOUR FAVORITE ANIME OR MANGA.

This one should be easy for every otaku. I mean I practically know everything about Hetalia, Black Butler, Katekyo Hitman Reborn, D.GrayMan, Ouran Host Club, and many more.

8. YOU SHALL FIGHT FOR ANIME.

Um….not really sure how to explain this, but yeah fight on for the name of anime! (Possibly about fighting to get a positive image on the name of anime instead of a weird one?)

9. YOU SHALL KNOW OPENING SONGS, ENDING SONGS, CHARACTER SONGS OF YOUR FAVORITE ANIME.

Basically like number seven, know all the songs for your favorite anime. I know I do.

10. YOU SHALL KNOW HOW TO SPEAK IN JAPANESE. (Even a little)

Ok this one you don't really have to follow but knowing some Japanese would be really cool to know. I know some Japanese I have been studying for at least 5 years now.

A Cosplayers Inspiration

Ok everyone has someone or something that inspires them to do things that make them happy. Like for instance people get inspiration from someone who they've always looked up too when growing up. This is also the same for cosplayers. I have many people that I look up to and most of them are cosplayers. My inspiration for cosplaying is the videos that I watched for hours on youtube, when I should have been doing my homework.

Those videos where made by the members of FightingDreamersPro and ParleProductions. I also know many people that have told me that I was the reason that they started cosplaying. All of those people just so happen to be my friends who I've met through the love of anime.

But having someone you look up to isn't the only way to be inspired to cosplay. Like for example the way anime is drawn and expressed through cosplay, is a way to be inspired or maybe you have been asked to go to an anime convention by your friend, and just seeing and feeling the friendly atmosphere is a good way too. Also it could be a promise that you made with someone who is dearest to you. There are many ways that cosplay inspires people to join this awesome social community.

NeoFang Summary

Ok, so in this chapter we talked about traits cosplayers should have, and again those traits are Manners, Patience, Resourceful, Focus, Dedication, Passion, Friendly, and Confidence. All cosplayer should remember these traits. We talked about what I call the Ten Commandments of an Anime Otaku. Cosplayers should follow these too. Yeah some of those sound stupid, but are really something that cosplayers go by. We also talked about how cosplayers have someone or something that inspired them to cosplay. But it's not just cosplayers, everyone has someone or something that inspires us. So now that's done let's move on to the next chapter.

Chapter Three

Hello cosplayers and welcome to chapter three, here we will discuss the different types of Lolita cosplayers, but before we get into the styles of lolitas we have to go over some Lolita history and how it ties in with visual kei. We will also talk about what types of cosplayers there are in general, and Visual Kei Fashion with a little bit of history, and the history of Harajuku.

The History of Harajuku

Harajuku is the name for the area around Harajuku Station on the Yamanote Line in the Shibuya ward of Tokyo, Japan. Every Sunday, people would dress in a variety of styles including gothic lolita, and visual kei, as well as cosplay and spend the day in Harajuku socializing. The fashion styles of these people rarely stick to one particular style and are usually a mesh of different styles.

Most people gather on the Jingu Bridge, which is a pedestrian bridge that connects Harajuku to the neighboring Meiji Shrine area.

Harajuku is also a fashion capital of the world, known for its unique street fashion. Harajuku street style is promoted in Japanese and international magazines such as Kera, Tune, Gothic & Lolita Bible and Fruits. Many prominent designers and fashion ideas have sprouted from Harajuku and have intertwined themselves into other fashions throughout the world.

Harajuku is also a large shopping district that includes international brands, its own brands, and shops selling clothes people can afford. Harajuku as it is now traces back to the end of World War II during the Allied occupation of Japan. U.S. soldiers and government civilians and their families lived in a nearby housing area called Washington Heights. It became an area where curious people flocked to

experience a different culture and stores in the area stocked goods marketed towards middle and upper class Japanese and Americans.

In 1958, Central Apartments were built in the area and were quickly occupied by fashion designers, models, and photographers. In 1964, when the summer

Olympics came to Tokyo the Harajuku area was further developed, and the idea of "Harajuku" slowly began to take a more concrete shape.

After the Olympics the people who hung out in the area, frequently referred to as the "Harajuku-zoku," or the "Harajuku tribe," began to develop a distinct culture and style unique to the area. From this distinct style grew the culture of Harajuku as a gathering ground for youth.

Visual Kei in general

Visual kei ("visual style" or "visual system") is a movement among Japanese musicians, that is characterized by the use of make-up, elaborate hair styles and flamboyant costumes, often, but not always, coupled with androgynous aesthetics. Some sources state that visual kei refers to a music genre, or to a sub-genre of Japanese rock, with its sound usually related to glam rock, punk rock and heavy metal. However other sources state that visual kei is only a fashion, with its unique clothing, make-up and participation in the related subculture being what exemplifies the use of the term.

Visual kei emerged in the mid-1980s, pioneered by bands such as X Japan, D'erlanger, Buck-Tick and Color. The term visual kei is believed to come from one of X Japan's slogans, "Psychedelic violence crime of visual shock". Color vocalist Dynamite Tommy formed his record company Free-Will in 1986, which has been a major contributor in spreading modern visual kei outside Japan.

Under Code Production, a sub-label of Free-Will founded by Kisaki, since its formation in 2003 has had a definite influence on newer independent visual kei bands, particularly in Osaka.

In 1992, X Japan tried to launch an attempt to enter the American market, but it fell through. It would take another 8 years until popularity and awareness of visual kei bands would extend worldwide. In the mid-1990s, visual kei received an increase in popularity throughout Japan, and album sales from visual kei bands started to reach record numbers.

The most notable bands to achieve success during this period included X Japan, Glay, and Luna Sea; however, a drastic change in their appearance accompanied their success. During the same period other bands, such as Kuroyume, Malice Mizer, and Penicillin, gained mainstream awareness, although they were not as commercially successful. By 1999, the mainstream popularity of visual kei was declining; X Japan had disbanded, and in 2000, Luna Sea decided to disband.

In 2007 the genre was revitalized, as Luna Sea performed a one-off performance, and X Japan reunited for a new single and a world tour. With these developments, visual kei bands enjoyed a boost in public awareness, described by some media as "neo-visual kei". New bands still use visual kei to describe themselves; some examples of current mainstream bands are Versailles, Nightmare, and The Gazette.

Visual kei has enjoyed popularity among independent underground projects, as well as artists achieving mainstream success, with influences from Western phenomena, such as glam, Goth and cyberpunk. The music performed encompasses a large variety of genres, i.e. punk, metal, pop and electronica. Magazines published regularly in Japan with visual kei coverage are Arena 37°C, Cure, Fool's Mate and Shoxx.

Noted bands that at least at some point sported a visual kei theme include Dir En Grey, Luna Sea and Malice Mizer. The popularity and awareness of such groups outside of Japan has seen an increase in recent years.

I am a Lolita Cosplayer, But hat type of Loli am I?

Just by looking at the title of this next section, your all probably thinking "What does she mean by Type of Lolita or Loli for short". Well I'll tell you exactly what I mean. There are many different types of lolitas, but before I get to into this subject I want to tell you a little bit about what a Lolita is.

Loli-History

Extravagant, Victorian-inspired clothing, curled hair, and doll-like makeup, sightings of these curious poppet's walking around the States, Europe and anime conventions. Take a vacation to Japan, particularly Tokyo's Harajuku district, and you are bound to face an army of these colorful and gothic dolls posing sweetly in the streets. Now, you may think you fell into Alice's rabbit hole and into a warped, gothic Wonderland, but in reality these fresh-faced darlings are part of a fashion subculture known as "Lolita." This Lolita fashion started in Japan during the late 70's, but took off in the 90's. Since, it has been passed through the world like a sugary, pink torrent. The fashion boasts a mix of Victorian and Rococo period clothing with more modern fashion trends like punk, goth and casual-wear.

Visual Kei and Loli-Fashion

Ok so I know that I talked about visual kei fashion already, but for this part I'm explaining how visual kei affects loli-fashion.

The rise of Lolita fashion was largely influenced by Japanese rock bands from the Visual Kei musical movement during the 80s and 90s. "Music is a major force in its creation," explains Chako Suzuki in her article "Pretty Babies: Japan's Undying Gothic Lolita Phenomenon, "Visual Kei is exactly as it sounds: Rock music that incorporates visual effects and elaborate costumes to heighten the experience of the music and the show." Of all the Visual Kei groups to advocate Lolita fashion the most notable was Malice Mizer, a band established in 1992. One of the two founding members, Mana, wore Gothic Lolita fashion.

Today he is a pioneer in the Lolita realm. Mana created one of the first and most lasting Lolita brands, Moi-Meme-Moitie. In doing so, he coined such terms as "Elegant Gothic Lolita" and "Elegant Gothic Aristocrat," fashions known for their dramatic gothic and sophisticated appeal in Lolita fashion. Today, Mana still is a well-respected and active force in Lolita Fashion, gracing the pages of the popular, seasonal Gothic & Lolita Bible magazine in his clothing-line.

Now you all have a good sense of Lolita Fashion. Now there isn't just one type of Lolita there are at least four types of lolitas and within those four categories are probably two to four sub-categories as well.

The first Loli is the Classic Lolita. A classic Lolita is a more aristocratic, mature style as it centers on Baroque and Rocaille fashion while using muted colors and patterns. The style in itself is not as dark as Gothic Lolita/Aristocrat or as juvenile and gaudy as Sweet Lolita.

♥ The Casual Lolita is a more toned down version of the style, while still retaining the basic lolita elements. It is very hard to put together a nice casual lolita co-ordination unless you have years of experience or are a natural at it. Most favored in the Casual Lolita co-ordination is (in a way) simplicity, so a nice simple cut-sew perhaps with a motif of some sort paired with a lolita skirt and hair accessory/headdress. (However the hair accessories are usually toned-down as well.) Casual Lolita can best be described as what a Lolita would wear when not 'dressing up.' Still modest and elegant, but not as over the top as most other Lolita styles. A great Casual Lolita can be compiled out of any color, as long as you remember to match colors, prints, etc. etc. as you would with any other Lolita style. A simple cardigan over a skirt creates a nice casual look.

The second Loli is one of my favorites, The Gothic Lolilta. The Gothic Lolita is a Lolita fashion with a dark edge. The style derives influence from Western Gothic subcultures like darker makeup, clothes and designs. However, Gothic Lolita maintains the frilly, Victorian sophistication of Lolita fashion.

For example, the style is more reminiscent of a

Victorian vampire like Dracula or Lestat from Anne Rice's

Interview with the Vampire, rather than Western gothic

figures like the Cure or Marilyn Manson. Gothic Lolita

fashion also uses crosses, coffins, bats, roses and other dark

characteristics in

its designs

♥ Shiro Lolita

(pictured side),

or 'White Lolita,'

is a Lolita outfit

made entirely of

white/cream/off-

white co-

ordinates. Shiro

Lolitas often pair themselves with Kuro Lolitas in twin

outfits to create an interesting contrast. Shiro Lolita can

be taken from any style of lolita, whether it be Gothic,

Sweet or Classic, if the co-ordination is completely

white then it is accepted as Shiro Lolita. PLEASE

NOTE: Wearing black shoes with a Shiro Lolita outfit

looks terrible

and is best to

be avoided.

♥ The Kuro

Lolita

(pictured on

side), or

'Black Lolita,'

like Shiro

Lolita, is an

outfit made-up of co-ordinates of one color, in this case;

black. Kuro also follows the same guidelines of most of

the other Lolita styles, so is still fairly easy to pull-off for beginners.

The third Loli is the Punk Lolita. Punk Lolita incorporates punk elements along with the class of Lolita fashion. These Punk fashion and its accessories include tattered clothing, chains, netting, safety pins, ties and screen-printed items. Hairstyles may be messy, dreads, colored and/or spikey.

And The Fourth and final Loli is The Sweet Lolita. The Sweet Lolita is just that: a sugar rush. Sweet Lolita exemplifies the youthful and doll-like side of Lolita fashion with frilly, colorful dresses, curled or straight hairstyles with bows and headbands, and modest makeup. Sweet Lolita accessories commonly involve lacey parasols, stuffed animals, and cute jewelry consisting of hearts, cakes and other cutesy objects.

♥ Hime Lolita, or 'Princess Lolita,' is a very elegant style of lolita that often involves miniature crowns, tiaras, and extravagant or large hair, and dresses. Because Hime Lolita does reflect a sense of royalty, and class, it is hard to pull this style off unless you are very well preened, and have done your best to look 'Princess-like. There is a fine line between Hime Lolita and the other styles as it is almost only defined by how you style yourself and not on the clothing. It is most common to see Hime Lolitas wearing Sweet Lolita dresses that have a Rococo influence. Any natural-looking make-up will look lovely with this style; just remember that the key is looking classy. Pearls, roses and bows suit this style perfectly.

♥ Country Lolita is derived from the Sweet Lolita style, and is often a little hard to distinguish due to the use of the same sweet patterns, and motifs that the Sweet Lolita style uses. How-ever the Country Lolita style can be recognized by straw baskets, hats, fruit, and gingham patterns. Most lolita outfits require a blouse under a jumper skirt to pull off the Lolita look, but because Country Lolita is associated with the out-doors one may be able to get away with-out a blouse. Like Sweet Lolita, Country Lolita follows the same modest guide-lines, as well as the full, bell-shaped skirt. The make-up suited for this style would be very basic, and natural. If you're going outside try some sun-screen, some light lip-stick, and some blush.

♥ Though this style of Lolita may seem like it should belong in a different category, I assure you that this Lolita is basically a cosplay styled Lolita. Sailor Lolita is a very nautical-themed style of Lolita that is very much inspired by Japanese Sailor-styled uniforms.

Sailor collars, dark blues, and whites are often key factors in recognizing this style. Nautical motifs are often used in this style; symbols such as ship anchors and wheels make very cute additions to this style. Like most Lolita styles the same bell-shaped skirt is expected, quite often this skirt may be pleated, and the outfit may often include a puffed-short-sleeved blouse with pockets. Although striped socks may not work with a lot of Lolita styles, they often look nice when coordinated into a Sailor Lolita outfit. Again minimal make-up with suit this style, including some lip-gloss to stop your lips from cracking if you'll be out near the sea!

Now there are some Lolita styles that aren't part of these four categories. But that doesn't mean that they're not Lolita styles, it just means their special. Like for instances the Kodona Lolita.

The Kodona Lolita is often called "boystyle" as it involves more masculine clothing. In Japan they usually use Ouji (meaning prince) and not Kodona, which is a western term. This style can be either laid back or very extravagant. Usually the people in this style are actually women and not men, but either can dress it. The men sometimes refer to themselves in this style as 'Dandy'.

Sometimes this style has feminine touches, such as more feminine shoes and accessories. Very common are 'prince pants' which are short Capri-style pants that cut off at the knee and usually have some details on them (such as lace-edged cuffs). Other common additions are suspenders, ties (regular ties and bowties), bowler caps and long socks (to cover the legs). Some of the more extravagant styles can include things like spats, canes, top hats, capes, etc.

But they keep the boyish part in tact so that they are not mistaken for Aristocrat. Hair is often in a boyish style, often shorter. Those with longer hair tend to put their hair in a less-girly way, such as hiding a bun under a cap. Makeup is often kept to a minimum, but sometimes darker makeup is applied around the eyes.

There is also one more category that I almost forgot about (Oops). That Category is called the Cosplay Lolita. You probably are thinking "what is she talking about, aren't all these categories of Lolita styles cosplays anyway?" NO! Cosplay Lolitas are completely different. Cosplay Lolita, or 'Costume Lolita,' is not a subset of Lolita fashion, but it is still important to know the difference between Cosplay Lolita and the actual fashion.

The Cosplay Lolita is often looked-down upon because it's usually seen at Anime Conventions being worn by those who don't really understand Lolita fashion and are happy to throw-on a costume quality ebay dress for the weekend. A lot of the time Cosplay Lolitas believes that Lolita is a costume instead of a fashion movement.

Cosplay Lolita generally doesn't conform to the actual standards of lolita fashion and usually includes very low quality materials, such as thin cottons or shiny fabric, synthetic raschel lace, satin ribbon, square-dance petticoats, cat/costume-ish ears, and poorly done corset-style lacing, stompy goth boots, lace gloves, low-quality colored wigs, leg warmers, stripper-esque high-heels, low-quality lace parasols, maid outfits, and short, un-modest skirts.

Cosplay lolita takes the lovable elements of Lolita fashion such as bows, lace, frills, and pushes them to the extreme, usually covering a dress with too many of these things, and entirely removing the classy image that most

Lolita fashion tries to convey. Make-up for this style can be anything from Mana-esque white-face, heavy eye-liner, thick goth eye shadow and black lipstick. And of course this category has many sub-categories.

♥ The Wa Lolita is a style that is often recognized by the Kimono-esque look of the outfits, and is for those Lolitas who may love to get in-touch with the country that brought about Lolita fashion. Wa Lolita involves long 'sode' or, sleeves, and 'obi' or sashes that are taken from Kimono/yukata outfits, and fused with the bell-shaped skirt of lolita. Wa Lolita fabrics are often very extravagant like most Kimono fabrics, involving detailed flower prints, and cranes. Like all Lolita outfits and Kimono, Wa Lolita should not be made out of shiny fabrics such as those that Chinese qi-pao are made of. Although this style is quite different from usual Lolita styles, modesty is still a large part of this style, and your skirt should be a reasonable length for lolita. Sadly a lot of Wa Lolita outfits on the market today have very short skirts, causing many people to be turned-off by Wa Lolita. Traditional Japanese Kanzashi or flower hairclips may work lovely with this style in the place of a Lolita head-dress. Make-up can range from light and natural to Japanese geisha inspired. It's best not to do makeup very similarly to that of a geisha as it will most likely end up looking costumey, and end-up ruining your beautifully put together outfit.

♥ The Guro Lolita (pictured on side) or 'Gore Lolita' is exactly what it is, gory. How gory is always up to you, and

can range

from

anything

to some

bandages,

a sling, or

some

blood

splatters

on your clothing. (Try not to over-do it though!)

Guro Lolita is a style of Lolita that tries to portray a 'broken-dolly' sort of look, a gruesome yet innocent sub-set of Lolita. A Guro Lolita outfit can really be pulled-off in any colour, but white really does look

fantastic if you want to have some blood splatters!
(If you're worried about getting blood splatters on
your lovely dress, perhaps you could make yourself
a small apron to splatter.) Make-up for this style is
really up to you, as long as you're still fairly modest
the sky is the limit. Fake blood is a great item to
have for this style, and can be purchased at a local
party store. And with that is a complete list of
different Loli styles.

So all you girls reading this section if you're choosing
to be a Loli-girl, then these styles are ones to choose from.
But you can favor more than one Loli style. I have at least
two Lolita styles that I like. What is important is that if you
choose…oh I don't know…. to be a punk Lolita, try not to
get gothic Lolita and punk Lolita mixed up. The two styles
are somewhat similar, so it is easy to get the two mixed up.

So just be careful. Okay enough on this topic, let's move to something else.

OK so I get the Lolita thing, but what about regular cosplayers? What type of cosplayer am I?

Oh my, that dreadful question, "what type of cosplayer am I?" Well I guess I should specify this question to "what types of cosplayers are there?" The answer to that is there is a wide range of cosplayers out there and are very specific too. What I mean by that is that most cosplayers tend to cosplay many characters, but there are cosplayers that cosplay only one character from a certain show. Others will cosplay many different characters from the same show until they end up cosplaying every single character in the particular show.

Like for instance, I happen to know someone that cosplays naruto and naruto only. I and the rest of AnimeRamenPro have made her watch many different anime shows, and in the end she likes them but will still only cosplay naruto. Anyway, let's move on to what this section is really about, basic types of cosplayer .

The first basic type is The Furries. Furries are cosplayers that dress up like anthropomorphic (humanized) animals. Yes, you all must be thinking "you mean those giant animals that have the huge eyes, giant heads and are everywhere at cons". Yes, that is exactly what I mean. Now a little thing you should keep in mind. Even though furries look kinda mean and kinda scary, and you can't really tell if there friendly or not because they are wear those giant heads and not showing their face, they are completely the opposite. Furries by far are the nicest and friendliest people I have ever met.

The second basic type is The Loli Cosplayers. I know exactly what you're thinking "Oh no, she's bringing that up again". Yes I am bringing it up again. Loli's are people who cosplay only in Lolita fashion. Though some Loli's cosplay characters from anime, but they make that character wear Lolita outfits (Which I personally think is quite funny).

I have seen many of those types of Loli's, but it's not a bad thing that they do that. It's really funny to see manly type of male characters like Zero from Vampire Knight or Naruto and Sasuke from Naruto in frilly dresses, and cute accessories.

The third basic type is what I am…half the time, The

Videogamers. The videogamers are (duh) people who cosplay characters that are from video games and spend most of their time playing video games. Some videogamers will cosplay and some will not, but that doesn't make them non-cosplayer.

It just means that they don't have the time and ability to make cosplays or they don't have /make enough money to buy cosplays. So keep in mind that cons are made for every type of cosplayers, not just ones that actually cosplay (remember that.)

The fourth is your average Cosplayer. They are known for cosplaying as your same sex characters meaning girls cosplay girls and boys cosplay boys. Not much to go in depth with.

The fifth which is what I am most of the time is a Crossplayer. A crossplayer is someone that cosplays as the opposite sex (Ex. girls cosplay boy characters) again not much to get into, except that when girls cosplay boys they bind their chest to get the look of a man's chest. Also they don't wear a lot of makeup, but they will wear at least a thin layer of eyeliner. Or they should at least.

And there you have it, the complete list of basic type cosplayers. Remember that though some of these types might not sound like "legit" cosplayers, they are. So don't think that you are better than them because you actually make or buy your cosplays and that you won many contest with your cosplays or something like that. Also remember that you can be more than one type of cosplayer, you don't have to choose one specific type. Let's move on to the summary!

<u>NeoFang's Summary</u>

We covered the topic of what are Lolita's and what are the different styles of Lolita's. And we see that there are a lot of different styles and many different sub-styles as well. What was also covered was the different types of cosplayers there are. And last we went over the history of Harajuku, and the History of Visual Kei and how the two tie together with each other as well as the style of Lolita. So let's get moving to the next chapter!

Chapter Four

Hello again cosplayers, and it looks like you made it through chapter three. Awesome, now let's get started with chapter four. In this chapter we'll go over cosplay construction, wig styling, make-up tips and basic sewing do's and don'ts.

<u>Sewing do's and don'ts</u>

Ok, if you are the kind of cosplayers that prefer to make cosplays instead of buying them (like me) then the first thing you need to do is have a reference picture and make a

list of the things you'll need for your cosplay, but there are some things you need to be aware of when buying fabrics, fabric paints, buttons, thread, Etc.

Color comparisons

For instance when you buy solid colored fabrics, make sure they are the exact color you need. For those of you that don't know what the heck I'm talking about, sometimes fabric may appear as the "right color" but that's when you take a closer look. Take the color black for instance, when you find the color black sometimes it will be like a smoky black type or ashy black type and that's when it's hard to tell.

Other fabric don'ts

Another thing to be aware of is a lot of fabric is made out of shiny material, you may think that making parts of your cosplay with shiny fabric is cool, but you might want to reconsider that thought. The reason you shouldn't use shiny fabric is because it will look weird in pictures, it will make you look like your clothes are glowing which do not want.

Ok we all know that there is more to sewing than just having fabric and a sewing machine. You also need to have thread.

Threads

Ok threads, oh how I hate this topic, but I have to talk about it sooner or later. Anyway thread is something that you must be careful with in sewing, especially the color. When choosing thread you should always get the same color thread as the fabric you're going to use. Black and white thread is one that you don't need to be real careful with, but you should keep in mind that if you are using lighter color fabric, you shouldn't use black (duh) because it will show in pictures and it won't look that good. Also make sure you have lots of bobbins, because I'm pretty sure you don't want to sit there for hours unwinding and rewinding the same two bobbins over and over, plus it would be a waste of good thread.

Needles!!!

Another thing is needles; from time to time your sewing machine will be a derp and will break your needle. So when that happens you will need to replace the needle, but there are different types of needles to choose from there are Denim Needles, Leather Needles, and Metallic Needles. So make sure you are using the right needle or else your stitching will look kinda funny, your thread will sometimes tangle and it will just be a pain untangling and it will take forever to finish. So to just sum this up have plenty of needles for different types of fabrics you use.

Patterns (last topic I swear)

Ok the last thing when you are making your cosplay, you'll need a pattern. I know, I know there are no specific patterns for the cosplay your making, that's when you have to find a pattern that looks almost like the cosplay then alter it. But when you find a pattern make sure it's one that is easy to alter or you will have a hard time putting the cosplay together.

Now real quick before we end this section, I want to just put a list of sewing supplies.

You'll need:

1. A sewing machine (duh)

2. Pins

3. Sewing machine needles

4. Measuring tape

5. A pattern that is similar to the style of your cosplay

6. Fabric and thread

7. Whatever accessories you will need

Now that we discussed all the sewing do's and don'ts now it's time to move onto the next section.

Cosplay Construction

The next section is cosplay construction. This section is a difficult one, so I will try the best I can to explain what this is about. I guess the first thing we'll discuss is choosing a cosplay. Ok first off there are three things to know about cosplay construction. First is Body type, two is sewing capability, and three is Money, yes this last one is very important.

Body Type

When choosing a cosplay you have to consider whether or not you can pull the character off. You have to consider whether or not you look like him/her, if you have the body type for that character. Knowing all that is probably the most important part about choosing a cosplay. Like take me for example, my body type is sort of in between I can pull off male and female characters.

My facial features are feminine, but I do have some boyish features. Some other body types are for cross dressers is for a girl with very maleish features, for those of you that have these types of features you want to stick around characters that are boys ranging from the ages of let's say 15-late 20's, or if you're like me and are in between then you should stick around female or male characters ranging from ages 15-late 20's.

If your body type is very feminine then definitely stick with younger teenage girl or younger boy characters. If you have sort of a "husky" body type like in big breasted or having those love handles and your facial features are feminine then you should stick to female characters ranging from ages late 20's to early 40's more or less.

But sometimes you choose a character you like, that's normally what everyone does but sometimes you should choose characters that you are not particularly fond of. Sure that doesn't sound like fun choosing a character you don't like but sometimes when you cosplay someone you don't like you come to respect them more.

Sewing Capability

Also when choosing a cosplay you have to consider whether or not you're gonna make the cosplay or if you want to have someone else make it for you, or if you have the time and patience to work on this. But the most important thing is if you have the sewing capability. Now when making a cosplay you really need to be sure that the character you choose is something you really want to spend your time and money on.

Also consider whether you have the time and skill to make the cosplay whether it is simple or really complex. Because no matter how simple the cosplay is, it will still be a challenge to first time cosplay constructers. Also consider whether or not you have the time to make every part of your cosplay including costume, wig, accessories, and props. Always ask yourself, do you have time before the con to make this cosplay, and do you have the patience to make this.

Also when making your cosplay buy fabric that's fit to wear at that con, like for instance if you are going to a con that is close to the winter season try to buy fabric that will keep you warm. Or if you are going to a con that is in the summer time choose fabric that isn't really heavy so that you don't sweat like crazy and feel uncomfortable for the whole day.

Money

Also consider the cost of all the materials as well, making cosplays isn't cheap. Now when your constructing a cosplay there will be times that there are some cosplay parts that are quite difficult to make. So you would have to buy the parts, but sometimes buying the parts isn't always the best thing to do. Like if you ordered a jacket it could either be too big or too small, because it wasn't fitted to you personally.

I got a purple gothic Lolita dress as a gift and it ended up being too tight around the chest area. I also ordered a Sebastian Michaelis cosplay from Black Butler and it was just a bit too tight around the sleeves so I can't really raise my arms when I wear this cosplay. That's why I prefer to make my cosplays myself, so if you want a cosplay that fits perfectly making it yourself is the best option. Also if you do decide to make your own cosplays, remember ALWAYS FOLLOW A PATTERN!!!! Trust me, making a cosplay without using a pattern will not turn out well at all.

Also when you start your cosplays, make sure that you have bought the right amount of fabric, so that you don't need to make another trip to the fabric store. Then you wash your fabric, and then you need to iron it. When cutting out your pattern pieces make sure that you pin them on the fabric so they don't move around when you cut them.

Also make sure you are cutting on the line. Believe me I've done that many times. Aside from sewing if you're making a cosplay using old clothes and adding stuff to it, don't be afraid to use iron on transfer paper and fabric paint. Believe me these things have saved my butt many times.

Other methods of obtaining cosplays

Cosplayers also obtain their cosplays through many different methods. Manufacturers produce and sell packaged outfits for use of cosplay, in a variety of qualities. These costumes are often sold online, but also can be purchased from dealers at conventions. There are also a number of individuals who work on commission, creating custom costumes, props or wigs designed and fitted to the individual; some websites for cosplay have classified ad sections where such services are advertised.

Other cosplayers, who prefer to create their own costumes, still provide a market for individual elements, accessories, and various raw materials, such as unstyled wigs or extensions, hair dye, cloth and sewing notions, liquid latex, body paint, face paint, shoes, costume jewelry and prop weapons. Most cosplayers engage in some combination of methods to obtain all the items necessary for their costume; for example they may commission a prop weapon, sew their own clothing, buy character jewelry from a cosplay accessory manufacturer, and buy a pair of off-the-rack shoes and modify them to match the desired look.

I almost forgot, Goodwill, Salvation Army, Flea Markets and Thrift stores are great places to find clothing for your cosplays. Items you find you can change to make it for your character.

Voice acting

Ok I'm not really a pro at this part; voicing your character is something that takes time and practice. I know it's easy to say the lines that character says, but the hard part is sounding like them, which is why I'm saying this now; if you want to voice characters, keep it in your voice range. It will be easier that way, especially for those who don't voice characters and are trying it for the first time. Like for instance, if a girl wants to cosplay oh I don't know France from Hetalia Axis powers, she would need to be able to pull off a somewhat realistic French accent while trying to sound male-ish.

Or if for some reason a boy wants to cosplay a female character like Grell Sutcliff from Black Butler,(yes I know Grell is a man but he says many times in both manga and show that he is a lady, but technically he's an "it" ^_^) he would have to make his voice sound very flamboyant and higher pitched. Lots of cosplayers go to panels to meet voice actors and ask the question "What got you started in voicing and what is a good way to get started in voice acting?" The answer to that question is to get practice in theater acting, gain the experience. Getting into voice acting is one way that cosplay can get you a job when people tell you that it can't. Now voice acting isn't a required thing to know how to do, but it sure is fun to learn how to do.

Wig Construction

Ok, Wigs in general are a pain to deal with, cause you can't decide whether or not to buy a styled wig or an unstyled wig so you could style it yourself. You don't know whether or not to order it now or later. Also wigs tend to be uncomfortable half the time (especially in the summer)! Also sometimes you ask yourself whether or not to get a wig for your costume or not. But let's be honest, wearing a wig can be fun too! I mean you can't really cosplay.....Sakura Haruno from Naruto if you have blonde hair when she has pink hair right?

Now on with a fun topic, wig styling ^_^. Wig styling is probably one of the hardest parts of cosplay construction (unless you buy a wig pre-styled). Now if you like to style wigs then there will be things you need like Hairspray, Hair glue, Hair dye (just trust me on that one), Hair putty, Etc.

If you have never styled wigs before, then when you buy hair products you need to research good hair products. I style all of my wigs and I have been using Got2b hair products for at least 5 years. But Got2b isn't the only hair product out there; there are a lot of good products like.

- ♥ Got2b
- ♥ TRESemme
- ♥ CHI
- ♥ BedHead

There will be a time that you just can't seem to find the perfect wig that you could style into your character's hair.

So what's the next thing to do is, buy a pre-cut wig then fix and style it. If you choose to do that remember that even though you bought it pre-cut, it wasn't cut on your head. So you would have to put the wig on and see what parts would need to be cut.

Where can I find good wigs?

You all are probably wondering, "Where can I find good quality wigs". Well that is a simple question and the answer is "to the internet!" seriously they're all over the internet but the best places to but wigs are:

- ♥ www.Ampfigory.com
- ♥ www.Ebay.com/cosplay/wigs
- ♥ www.cosplay.com/wigs
- ♥ www.Epiccosplay.com

These sites are the sites that I use for my wigs and so far I have been really happy with the quality and how much easier it is to style them. Also another thing that should be done is watch videos on how to cut and style a wig for your character and that character alone. Watching those will help with how to layer the hair and how to create the style, like if your character has really spikey hair. Also have plenty of reference pictures for your character when styling.

Makeup tips

Ok this topic isn't one of my favorites to talk about, but I have to. Sometimes cosplayers will wear makeup to give them a more anime look, but most cosplays require makeup because it completes the character. You all are probably thinking "Oh no, I hate wearing makeup, or I don't look good in makeup". Well I admit I don't look that good in makeup either but, I still wear it for my cosplay. So it wouldn't hurt to try it right ^_^.

First when putting on makeup you should always wash your face, and then when removing makeup wash your face again. Because if you're someone that gets really bad acne, some types of makeup will cause you to break out a lot. Once you wash your face then start with a light moisture crème it will not only protect your skin, but it will also keep the makeup on longer. Next you apply either powder or liquid makeup.

Powder makeup is easy to apply and isn't blotchy, but the problem with powder makeup is it wears off faster than liquid makeup. Liquid makeup does come on thicker, but it doesn't make your face reflect a lot of sunlight, which is great when taking pictures outside. I don't use this but, concealer is something that you should use if you have bad acne, dark spots, and dark circles under your eyes.

Lips

Here is a little trick I found about how to cover up cracked lips, Use sugar and honey on your lips before anything! Combine a little bit of honey and lots of sugar in a small container, and then rub it in! Then remove with a warm wash cloth. It really does help with the overall look, nobody likes cracked lips yuck! And after you use that use CHAPSTICK, NOT LIPGLOSS, then lipstick or whatever.

If you're a girly girl use a shimmer over pink lipstick (ex. Lolitas/ Dolly/ Fairy Kei) little bit of red blended for general girl cosplay. NUDE lipstick for crossplaying boys! (Or concealer) Deep red or black for more dramatic characaters.

Eyebrows

If you have more thick eyebrows like me, use concealer first then wait for it to dry a little. After put on a white glue stick nontoxic of course and be sure it's washable this will keep your hair down, NO SUPER GLUE! After, trace your eyebrows using eyeliner. This is only if you are just making your eyebrows look thinner, if you have a character with eyebrows of a different color like let's say red, white, or blonde, then you would use eye shadow of the color you need and trace out you eyebrow to look like the character's.

If you have more thin eyebrows, use a little glue on the insides of your eyebrows. After it's dry-ish, use eye shadow to shape you eyebrows. And again if you need them to be a different color, find eye shadow in the color that you character's eyebrows are.

Eye makeup

For girls cosplaying male characters remember guys don't usually wear makeup, unless you're a gay character that wears makeup, or drag queen. But it's still ok to wear some makeup to bring out the eyes a little.

1.   A thin line of eyeliner (Black), you don't want too much eyeliner because guys don't usually wear eyeliner

2.   A little mascara (Black)

For girls cosplaying female characters, you definitely should wear makeup, not only will it make your eye look more anime-ish, it will make your character more feminine. Which is the whole point.

1.   A small line of eyeliner, you could use pencil or liquid.

2.   Mascara

3. If you want, use fake eyelashes

4. Never share eye makeup

5. Also if you want to, use eye shadow. Just don't use colors that don't really go with the cosplay unless it calls for different colors. If you use eye shadow, use light colors like pink, silver, black, grey or white or you could go by this:

Wig ~ Color eye shadow

Pink ~ Grey

Green ~ Pink

Blue ~ Green

Red ~ Black

Brown ~ Blue

Black ~ White

Purple ~ Yellow

Yellow/Blonde ~
Brown

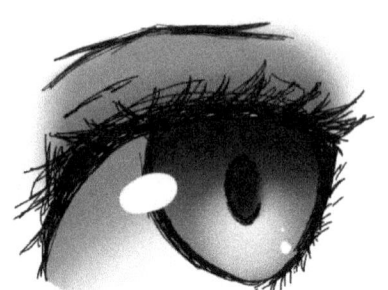

Body Makeup

Some cosplays require body makeup, like the trolls from HomeStuck. Their skin is grey so you would need grey body paint. Other characters have tattoos like Dino from Katekyo Hitman Reborn. He has tattoos on his left arm (I think). Now if you cosplay a character with tattoos, that doesn't mean you have to go out and get a tattoo (unless you want to if you really like that character. For younger cosplayers, I would not suggest getting one, I don't think your parents would approve).

The best way to make the tattoo is to draw it on your body. You could use makeup or markers (I say markers because lots of people like to draw on themselves with markers anyway. So it works ^_^). There are websites that sell body paint, theatrical latex, and all sorts of different theatrical products. Like for instance WWW.fxsupply.com. This website has lots of stuff for fake cuts and scars, also for different facial features.

Now when it comes to using body paint like let's say you wanted to cosplay any of the trolls from Homestuck, you would need to cover any showing skin in grey body paint. It might seem strange to wear body paint; especially when you want to cosplay outside of a con, you will start to feel a little weird about going out in public covered in grey body paint.

Trust me, it's not weird at all, I do this a lot. Sure it was weird at first because people were staring and saying things about me, if you are serious about being a cosplayer you can't let things like that bother you. Being a cosplayer is all about expressing yourself through your cosplays. You can't let little things like that stop you from being who you are. (Yeah, I realize that this is kinda getting off track of the topic body makeup, it's also something that goes with any topic in this book including this topic).

Contacts

If your that kind of cosplayer that wears colored contacts, and you don't wear contacts normally then you need to be really careful when buying contacts and wearing them. Now when buying contacts you need to make sure that the contacts lifespan is either 90 days or a 1 year. Also make sure that the website you buy from is FDA approved as well. For younger cosplayers that want to wear colored contacts, I would advise asking a parents permission and talk about buying it before you buy them. Doctors recommend that nobody under the age of 13 should wear contacts, so always ask your eye doctor if contacts are right for you.

If you bought a pair (this is the part you should pay attention to if you are someone that has never worn contacts before), have someone show you how to put them in or what I did was find YouTube video's on how to put them in. I say this because if you put them in wrong, one it will hurt, and two you could cut your cornea and you will go blind. Always make sure that your contacts are right side out when putting them in as well, they should look like a half sphere, not a lipped bowl. So please, PLEASE be careful. One other thing to remember is that you NEVER share contacts, because you could get eye infections. Also be sure to carry around a contact case and contact solution just in case your eyes get irritated. Eye drops are another must have if you are prone to dry eyes, or your eyes start to get a little sore. Another thing about buying contacts is the different types of contacts. There are a lot of different types of contacts but I will only list three

- ♥ Visibility tints: This is usually a light blue or green tint which is added to a lens. It is designed to help you see the lens better when inserting and removing contacts, or in case you drop one. Since it is a very light tint, a colored lens with a visibility tint does not affect your eye color.

- ♥ Enhancement tints: This is a solid, but translucent (see-through) tint that is a little darker than a visibility tint. An enhancement tint lens is different as it doesn't change your eye color. As the name implies, its purpose is to enhance the existing color of your eyes. These are usually recommended for contact lens wearers who have light colored eyes and want to intensify their eye color.

♥ Color tints: These lenses are deeper tints that change your eye color completely. Color tints typically consist of patterns of solid colors. If you have dark eyes, this is the type of lens that will be necessary in order to change your eye color. Color contacts come in a wide variety of colors, including hazel, green, blue, purple and gray.

For cosplayers with brown eyes

For those of you who have brown eyes keep in mind that you should buy solid color contacts. Because if you buy contacts that blend with your natural eye color, the color won't show. So always remember that when buying contacts.

Putting in contacts

The first thing you must do before putting in contacts is to wash your hands. You have to make sure that nothing is on your hands. Then wipe your hand down with the contacts solution, and then rub the contact in a circular motion to clean it, because if you don't clean the contact then you could possibly be putting in bacteria in your eyes. Then you put the contact on your finger and pull the top eye lid up and bottom lid down the place the contact on your eye. Sometimes it won't go in right away (it helps if you dry off the finger that you are using to put it in on a paper towel so that the contact will go right for the liquid in your eye and not stick to the liquid on your finger!), so don't get mad just keep trying until it stays on your eye.

Now when you take them out, you pull the bottom lid down and gently slide the contact toward the bottom lid.

Then you pinch the contacts and pull it out. Always make sure you clean your contact after every time you wear them or bacteria will build up and mess up the contact and you could really hurt your eyes.

Neofang's Summary

Ok in this chapter we went over sewing do's and don'ts, like color comparison, needles, patterns, and all that good stuff. We went over cosplay construction and how knowing your body type well enough to say "can I pull this cosplay off". We also went over makeup tips for cosplayers, and we went over wig construction, where to get good wigs and what hair products are good for styling. And how to use contacts. Now let's move on shall we?

Chapter Five

Ok cosplayers, welcome to chapter five. In this chapter we will discuss tips for first time con-goers, cosplay do's and don'ts, and Helpful Panels to look out for. This is where things get interesting.......I think.

<u>Tips for first time con-goers</u>

Ok in this section I want to talk about tips that first time cosplayers should know for when they go out to their first con. This list isn't very long so let's get started shall we?

1. First thing you should have with you when you go to your first con is a first aid kit. I know that that sounds kind of strange but, it will be good to have one with you because you never know what is going to happen. It might not be you but there will be someone around you that could get

hurt. So having a first aid kit is always good. (Just don't do what I do, by telling others and your readers to pack one and forgetting to bring one when a con comes around.)

2. Next is a mini travel size sewing kit. Along with your kit it's good to have a spool of thread that matches your cosplay. The reason for wanting to have a mini sewing kit is because again you'll never know what could happen. You could possibly trip, fall and rip you cosplay, or your cosplay could magically start coming undone at the seams. Trust me; this has happened to me lots of times. Also, always have safety pins. Safety pins are good because let's say if you don't have time to sew up a tear in your cosplay, you can just pin it up with a safety pin. They are always good to have when you have small pieces to pin on your cosplay too.

3. Ok this one is a BIG must have when you go to cons; always bring one of those travel kits that have the shampoos, conditioner, toothpaste, and <u>deodorant</u>!!! Never forget to bring deodorant, because cons will either be outdoor cons or summer cons and you will get hot and sweaty. Just because you're away from your home for three days, does not mean you don't have to shower. Believe me no one wants to stand next to you in line while waiting to get in to an event if your smelling like con funk.

Also, another thing that you should have is oil- free makeup wipes. These are good for cleaning off any makeup from your cosplay. It's good to have these, or you would have makeup just being piled on for three days of the cons.

4. Research, Reasearch, RESEARCH!!!! This something you want to do if this is your first con. First you find cons in your area; a good place to look is

animecons.con which has every con listed throughout the world. Next decide whether you want to attend a huge con or small con. Large cons can have anywhere between 15 to 40 thousand people attending, so make sure you're up to it.

At a large convention, there is no way you'll be able to attend every event, so keep this in mind. On the flip side, big cons always have the most famous bands and guest artists. Some cons have a higher cover fee than others, and you may want to take this into consideration. Make sure that your con takes place at a time when you will be able to vacation for 3 days. Also if you plan on attending cons out of state do research for hotels in the area of the con and how much it would cost you so that you can start working on a budget.

♥ This is also very important, make sure that if you're staying in a hotel make sure you have a separate budget, so that you don't end up spend all your money that you need to pay for your room. Most hotels normally have you pay at checkout, so this would be a good way not to over spend on a con and then have money problems later. Also if you have others staying with you, have them help with room cost. That way you save money and have extra spending money.

5. Decide how you're going to get there. If it's far away, are you going to fly? If you're planning on a road trip, will you rent a car? Who will drive it? How much will gas cost? Make sure you have more than one person who can drive, and that the car you've chosen is reliable and has enough room in it for the passengers and luggage. Figure out who you are going to take with you, if anyone.

6. Register early. The price of con registration goes up the closer you get to the day of, with usually a difference of

$15-$20 between the early price and the at-con price. If you pre-register, all you have to do is pick up your badge the night before or the morning of the con, and it saves everyone a lot of stress. At-con registration is expensive, stressful, and usually involves getting up at 5:30 am (depending on how far away you are from the con) to avoid standing in a long line of other people who also forgot to pre-register. Usually registration for a con opens up about three months before it occurs, so be ready.

♥ Bring enough spending money. Remember to bring spending money too! You can easily spend more than $200 dollars at con on clothing, posters, DVDs, books, and other merchandise. You will be very sad if you get to the con with your $25 and want to buy some souvenirs, and don't have enough money. So come prepared! Books and DVDs are sometimes discounted, so there's incentive to buy them there.

7. Know if you are you going to cosplay. If so, plan in advance. Buy or start making your costume at least four months in advance. That way it's sure to be shipped on time if you're ordering it, or you'll have plenty of time to sew it. Even if you sew every day for hours, it still takes two or three weeks to make even a simple costume, so give yourself enough time.

8. Ok now I also want to talk about when packing for a con. When you pack always have more than a back pack or suit case. Bring a back pack and a suit case, the suit case would be good for carrying cosplays and extra clothes, and the back pack would be good for carrying stuff like makeup, computers, and most importantly the stuff that you buy ^_^.

I know it just sounds like a lot more weight to carry to your car, but it is actually better to have both a huge suit case and back pack then just having a back pack or just a suit case. I mean I sometimes see cosplayers come out of their cars on day one of the cons carrying their cosplays up to their rooms on hangers alone. I think to myself that it would be much easier for them if they had a bag to put them in.

♥ Take cosplay into consideration when packing, too. Think of how much space your costume and accessories need, and make sure you have that space. Are any of your travel mates doing large, bulky cosplays? Find out!

♥ Bring a sewing kit, duct tape, permanent markers, and/or whatever else you need to make emergency costume repairs. If your costume tears or breaks you'll be very sad if you can't fix it!

♥ If you're cosplaying, practice poses in costume beforehand. That way you'll be ready to strut your stuff when people ask to photograph you - and they will if your cosplay is halfway decent!

♥ Make sure your costume is appropriate for a potentially crowded con. Try to avoid long trailing pieces of clothing that could easily be stepped on or large accessories on your back that could hit people as you turn around. Your costume should allow you to move around easily and see reasonably well. If your costume does limit your vision, recruit a friend to escort you around the con or just try to stay in one place while you're wearing it.

9. Give yourself plenty of time to get there if you live more than a couple hours away. You don't want to get there at midnight the night before, or even worse, 6 am the morning of! Make sure you have time to settle into your hotel room and get a good night's sleep the night before. You'll need your energy!

10. Read the con guide before you go. At registration, you are given a booklet containing con rules, as well as a detailed schedule of events. Take a couple minutes to run through this with a highlighter pen and mark anything that catches your eye. This way you won't miss any of your favorite anime screenings, autograph sessions, or band performances. Also make sure that if you are with others, make sure to plan with them.

Don't worry about planning every minute. Just find out what interests you beforehand and make your decisions as you go. Do not try to attend everything that interests you! It isn't possible, and rushing around all day to catch five minutes of everything will just make you feel tired and dissatisfied.

11. Do not be afraid to split up. If you're at con with friends, don't feel pressured to spend every minute with

them. Set up a designated time and place to meet, then go off to explore on your own or in pair if you're part of a large group. Cons have something for everyone, and no matter how much you and your friends have in common, you won't all want to do the same thing all of the time!

12. Line up early for big-name events. For band performances, cosplay and AMV contests, and awards ceremonies, make sure you get there early. Lines can grow to epic sizes, and although chatting with fellow attendees in line can be fun, waiting 45 minutes to an hour is not.

13. And the last and final tip is making sure you give yourself enough time to leave and get home. You may be tempted to stay until late into the night on the last day of con, but if it's a Sunday and you have school or work the next day, you may want to reconsider. By the last day, the

important events are usually over, so don't feel bad about skipping out on the last half-day if you have to get home.

14. Oh and one more thing don't forget to eat lunch and dinner, even if it's just grabbing a quick bite at the con's hotel or convention center. Staying till midnight to catch a late night anime showing can be fun, but don't stay into the wee hours every night and wake up groggy and exhausted in the morning, also remember to eat breakfast: even if it's just pop tarts or muffins.

Ok enough of this let's move on to something else shall we?

Cons do's and don't's

Ok this section is all about what to do at cons and what not to do at cons. Yeah so with that said let's get started with the Don'ts.

Don'ts

1. Ok the first don't is <u>do not touch the props</u>! This is a major don't, cosplayers work hard to make these props or spent a lot of money on them and they don't want people taking their props and breaking them. So I say again <u>don't touch the props</u> unless you were given permission by the owner of said prop first.

2. Next, don't be rude and obnoxious. We all want to have a good time so, don't be the one to ruin it by being rude and obnoxious. Use your manners and please keep the horse play to a safe border line of over the top horse play to boring, almost just standing there doing nothing.

3. Next, don't go up to people and hug them without asking. People will look at you like "why are you touching me, get off." so please just ask before you hug someone.

4. Also, please always remember this. <u>Do not</u> go up to people and do what I call "playful sexual harassment". Meaning, don't randomly pelvic thrust someone, don't go up to someone and "fist" them. Please awkward moments are something we all want to avoid.

5. As much fun as this sounds, don't glomp (a glomp is a hug in which you tackle the person). . Glomping can really hurt someone, so please think about it before you do

it. You will never know if someone has something wrong with them. Beside most cons have glomping banned.

6. Don't cosplay for the sake of entering contests and winning. Cosplay is supposed to be a fun hobby for everyone, not a competition.

7. Don't treat others as inferior to you just because the quality of their cosplays isn't at its peak. Cosplayers are all equal. This also goes with this; don't think you are the only one that cosplays that character or the "best" at the character. There are others that cosplay the same character, believe it or not, and no one is better than anyone else. Again, we are all equal.

8. Don't overuse the glue gun. Yes, this fabulous invention is great in a jam or for some construction, but it does start to look messy and unprofessional if you use too much. So if you want a good looking cosplay don't go

overboard on hot glue, especially if you are at the con and need a cosplay repair.

9. Ok now this is a HUGE don't. Never cosplay a character that normally complains to start drama with a certain individual. Please never do this, because you will not only make the weekend horrible for the other person, but everyone at the con will think that all you do is start drama, and no one will talk or hang out with you for the rest of the con.

So if you don't want this to happen, don't use cosplay as an excuse to start drama. Not only will you be labeled as drama starter for that weekend but throughout the anime community will spread your name to every social media site, and make people aware that you are a drama starter. We all want to have fun so don't ruin it for others.

Ok now let's start with the Do's. There's not much but I will still talk about them ^_^. Now there are some of these do's that are pretty big and really should be kept in mind when you are at a con especially if it's you first con.

Do's

1. Always use your manners. I can't stress this enough. I run into rude people at cons from time to time. Please use your manners, especially in the dealers room.

2. Have Fun, it's good to have fun, we all like to have fun. Not too much fun though, you don't want to hurt yourself (lol). Also remember to take PICTURES!!!! You

want to take pictures to have memories of you in your cosplay at the time, and of you with the people you meet.

3. Make Friends, making friends at cons is probably the best way to make friends. Remember to get your new friend's face book and maybe even their phone number.

4. Do study the character's mannerisms-pay close attention to how the character carries himself/herself. This also known as staying in character, always stay in character.

5. Do have at least 3 different poses. This is where the studying comes in. Find poses that you feel expresses the character best. Don't do random poses that you don't see the character doing. Don't do happy type poses for a character that is either angry or sad most of the time.

6. Do try to bring the character to life. You never know-you might make someone's day. Now normally that's something you want to do. But if you are the kind of person that has trouble with this; just stop trying and let it come naturally. Most of the time just not even trying to be in character, you somehow fall into that character.

7. Do try to have a reference image of every angle. If this isn't possible (like in the case of an artbook image), use your better judgement of the other angles. Add your own flare to the costume, but keep it as close to character as you can.

Now that all the do's and don'ts have been listed, let's move on. But before we do, always remember these when you are at any con, especially the ones about how to bring the character out of the anime into real life.

Panels

Ok this section is about panels, you know those shows that are Q and A in these rooms at cons. Not all panels are Q and A; there are a wide range of panels, like random comic type shows and skits. There are some panels that offer some useful tips for cosplayers. Like cosplays on $50 and $75 budgets or good techniques for wig styling.

The most common panel subjects are Prop Construction. Prop Construction panels basically show you how most people make props or armor for certain characters. They sometimes bring in some armor and props that they've built for show. Another common panel is a Q and A panel. In a Q and A you would normally have a row of cosplay either dressed in cosplay or cosplayers in their normal every day wear, and you ask them questions either for them or for the character they're cosplaying.

Then they will answer you with a serious answer or a funny answer. Now there are some panels that aren't about cosplay tips or Q and A, there are panels like for instance BJD 101, these panels also good to look out for if you are a BJD lover. These panels show you all the different types of BJDs from height to doll brand.

They show how to do face-ups if you are the kind that would prefer to do it on your own so that you have a

personalized dollfie. (Oops maybe I should explain what a BJD is >w< ;.) Ok BJD stands for Ball Jointed Dolls or they are also known as Dollfies, these dolls are normally made out of a plastic material called resin and are strung together with very thick elastic. These dolls are almost considered to be porcelain dolls.

These dolls are also know for how life like they are. The way that someone does a BJD's face up (makeup) is incredible. These dolls range in sizes from 60cm which is known as a Super Dollife or SD for short, 40cm known as Mini Super Dollfie or MSD, and 10cm known as Tiny Dollfie or TD. There are also many different types of BJDS. There are Volks, Luts, D.I.M (Doll in Mind), Dollshe, D.O.D (Dream of Doll), and Bobobie.

Now you don't always have to attend every panel because some are at the same time as others. Also when you are in a panel room; don't be rude and shout out random things during a skit or when someone is asking or answering any questions. There are also panels that you can be interactive with. Like for instances interactive panels are panels that involve the crowd. Normally you would have a group of people that will perform a skit while they bring in others from the crowd to help them in their performance. Of course they would pick someone and they would already know what to do. The performers would give them certains parts to act out even if they have no script to follow, so they would just wing it and do improv. There are also role playing panels and LARP panels.

If you don't know what those are, Role Playing panels are when the people running the panel are doing a skit and they ask people from the audience to join in on the skit. These types of panels are somewhat similar to interactive panels. LARP panels are Live Action Role Playing, which is when someone brings foam weapons and you go one on one with someone until you have been hit. If you decide to go to these types of panels don't be shy, go and have fun.

NeoFang's Summary

Ok so we discussed tips for first time cosplayers. Yeah there are a lot of tips but they are very useful, especially if you are staying in a hotel for the first time. We listed all the do's and don'ts of cons. We also talked about types of panels that are helpful to cosplayers and BJD lovers and panels that are interactive. Well it seems we are coming to the end of our fun journey, but before we come to an end. Let's move on to one last thing shall we?

Cosplayers of the future and the future in General (brace yourself world)

Ok before I bring this to an end, this is something I wanted to save for the end. People say that you only live once or YOLO, but no matter what, just think of this when you're older, I'm not too old for this, I'll never be too old for this. Also think of this too, when I die I want to die doing what I loved doing, whether it's cosplaying, drawing, singing, playing an instrument, or dancing, etc.,the list goes on and on.

But never ever say you're too old for anything, even if it's cosplaying cause that means you're just giving up on what you did best expressing yourself. Even if the world comes to an end, don't ever stop doing what you do best no matter what it is.

As for the future of cosplayers (that's a scary thought), all I can see for us is that we have a lot of new and exciting worlds of cons to explore and many new friends to make. I bet many cosplayers share this same wish, that one day cosplaying will be accepted as an exciting new way to express one's self, instead of being that weird teenaged hobby that everyone is involved in. I hope that one day society will be more open about cosplayers, including parents or any family members in general, and people that are not as involved in cosplaying that like to make fun of us.

I asked this question on deviantArt a few months ago asking "what cosplay means to you," I got a few very interesting replies, but not a lot. Here's what some of those replies were:

♥ Words from Victoria:

To me, so far, it means showing a love for being a nerd, challenging what the teenage "norm" says we should be, and getting to spend time with the friends that don't get embarrassed when they hang out with me!

♥ Words from Mia:

I agree with what auzie-angel said. Cosplaying to me means that you are not afraid to stand out from other "normal" teens.

♥ Words from Katie:

It means to me, just dressing up like someone else, and it makes me really happy when I'm cosplaying with my friends.

♥ Words from Sam:

To me, it's being people that you want to be and having fun.

♥ Words from Maddie:

For me, cosplaying is getting the experience being someone you know you can't be, and being with your friends experience all this with them.

♥ Words from Julia:

It means just going crazy and doing whatever you want because you are being someone else when you do.

♥ Words from Jordan:

Cosplay to me is, a show of appreciation for your favorite characters

♥ Words from Raven:

Cosplay to me is a freedom of expression because every day is like Halloween and a chance to be someone different.

♥ Words from Justin:

There's something special about cosplay, you feel good about it. You make that costume (usually), you put in a lot of hard work, and then you become that character. It's something truly fun to do. Even if you do get strange looks from time to time!

Ok, people have many different ways of looking at cosplay. But no matter how differently we explain it, the answer is always the same. Just having fun and being with friends that share the same feelings. Now you're all probably wondering, what I think cosplay means to me. For me cosplay means, no matter how different you are to others around, you know that outside of school, or work, or wherever, you know there are tons of people just like you in a place where we all come together to have fun.

There is no such thing as normal; everyone has their own normal, which could seem weird in other's eye. I'm proud to be called weird, or a nerd. I'm glad to call myself a cosplayer and all of you should be too!

Thank you all for being such awesome people, I have been shown a lot since I started cosplaying, have had so many critiques on my cosplays, artworks, and props that I've made, and with all of those it made me a much better cosplayer than before. I still have a lot to learn even though I wrote this, but there is never an end to cosplay knowledge.

Now, I hope that this book was very helpful for all of you cosplayers whether you are newbies or veterans, and if you are thinking about attending your first con, make it the best con you've ever been to. And who knows, maybe one day we will meet each other at one and make memories together. So until then sayonara, and thanks for joining me

at Cosplay Academy.

Meet the Author

My name is Harloe I. Hunter; I'm a cosplayer and have been one for going on 5 years now. I am mostly known for being the spastic founder of AnimeRamenProductions. I've been to at least 15+ conventions, all in the state of Florida, and I have made over 20 cosplays also including quick put togethers. I have cosplayed Naruto Uzumaki, Hinata Hyuuga, Sasuke Uchiha, Allen Walker, Hikaru Hitachiin, Mori-sempai, Sora, Near, L, Edward Elric, Izaya Onihira,

China, Prussia, Tsuna Sawada, Karkat Vantas, Dave and Baby Dave Strider, Nepeta Lejion, John Egbert, Sebastian Michaelis, Raichu, Len Kagamine, Ellis from L4D2, Rin Okumura, and many more (did so many I can't remember the rest). I have been drawing fanart and been writing fanfics for as long as I have been cosplaying.

I lived in Sparta New Jersey, and then by the time I was eight I moved to Florida. I started cosplaying back in fifth grade and went to my first cosplay con back in 2008. By the time I got into middle school my whole cosplay social life had already taken its roots. When I started middle school I thought that I was gonna be the only anime nerd there, but I was wrong.

I made some of the best anime pals at middle school and we continue at high school since our middle school was also a high school and always will be even, after we graduate in 2015. Anyway, these friends always tell me and still tell me that I was the reason for them cosplaying.

I brought them to many cons, and for some of them it was their very first con. The moment they walk through the convention doors their eyes light up with excitement. That will always be my favorite memory of when they went to their first con with me. I love it when I can take friends that love anime, but have never been to a con and make their life complete. I love when I can have any chance to help my friends make there cosplays, these feelings are like the best feelings a cosplayer could ever have.

It reminds me of myself when I first started going to cons, I was young and a newbie cosplay and seeing all these people with really well done cosplay, was just truly amazing. Then when I really got into it and when I made friends that really loved anime and couldn't go to cons and

experience the whole atmosphere because their parents
didn't like the whole idea of dressing up and hanging with
weirdos. I felt the urge to help them feel that experience; I
felt the urge when my friends would say that they really
wanted to make their first cosplays to help them with their
cosplays. Well besides when you go to a brand new con,
meaning the cons very first year.

Oh if you all are wondering why I didn't do this in the
beginning it's because I can ^_^.